THE WAR ON FREE SPEECH

THE WAR ON FREE SPEECH

VICTOR BLACKTHORN

CONTENTS

First Printing, 2025

Introduction: Why Free Speech Matters

The Foundation of Democracy

Free speech is the cornerstone of any democratic society. It allows people to share ideas, question authority, and engage in open debates that lead to progress. Without free speech, democracy weakens, as governments and powerful entities can silence opposition and control information. Throughout history, societies that have protected free speech have thrived, while those that have suppressed it have suffered from oppression and stagnation.

One of the key roles of free speech is holding leaders accountable. When people can freely criticize those in power, corruption is exposed, and better policies emerge. Without this freedom, governments can operate in secrecy, making decisions that benefit the few rather than the many. Free speech also ensures that individuals have the right to express their beliefs, opinions, and ideas without fear of punishment. This protection fosters creativity, innovation, and social progress.

A Right Under Threat

Despite its importance, free speech is under attack in many parts of the world. Governments, private corporations, and even social movements are imposing restrictions on what people can say. In authoritarian regimes, dissent is met with imprisonment or even violence. However, even in democratic nations, free speech is being curtailed through new laws, social pressures, and the influence of major tech companies.

Online platforms, which were once seen as spaces for open expression, now engage in censorship through content moderation policies, deplatforming, and algorithmic suppression of certain viewpoints. Many journalists, activists, and everyday individuals have been silenced for sharing opinions that challenge mainstream narratives. This growing trend raises serious concerns about who gets to decide what is acceptable speech and what is not.

The Consequences of Silence

When free speech is restricted, the consequences are severe. Suppressing open discussion prevents the truth from being discovered, leading to misinformation and manipulation. Without diverse viewpoints, society loses its ability to solve complex problems, as only one-sided perspectives are allowed to be heard.

A loss of free speech also results in the erosion of personal freedoms. When individuals fear speaking their minds, self-censorship takes hold, creating a culture where people are afraid to question authority or express unpopular opinions. This fear leads to widespread public mistrust, as people no longer feel they have a voice in shaping their communities or governments.

A Call to Action

Protecting free speech is not just the responsibility of governments or media organizations—it is everyone's duty. If society fails to defend this fundamental right, future generations will inherit a world where open debate is replaced by controlled narratives.

This book will explore the many ways in which free speech is being threatened and why it must be preserved. By understanding the dangers of censorship and the importance of open dialogue, we can work together to ensure that the right to express ourselves freely remains protected. The fight for free speech is a fight for democracy itself, and it is a battle we cannot afford to lose.

CHAPTER 1

Chapter 1: The History of Free Speech

Ancient Beginnings

The concept of free speech dates back thousands of years, with some of the earliest examples found in ancient civilizations. In ancient Greece, democracy flourished in the city-state of Athens, where open debate was encouraged in the public assembly, known as the Ecclesia. Citizens had the right to voice their opinions on laws, policies, and leadership, shaping the course of governance. Philosophers like Socrates engaged in critical discussions about morality, governance, and justice, emphasizing the importance of questioning commonly held beliefs.

However, even in Athens, free speech had its limits. Socrates himself was sentenced to death in 399 BCE for allegedly corrupting the youth and questioning the gods, demonstrating that even the birthplace of democracy struggled with the balance between free expression and societal norms. While Athens promoted debate, controversial ideas could still be met with harsh consequences.

Rome also played a role in shaping free speech. The Roman Republic allowed senators and citizens to voice their opinions in the Forum, influencing policies and governance. Public discourse was an essential part of Roman political life, with orators like Cicero using speech to challenge corruption and advocate for reform. However, as Rome transitioned into an empire, speech became more restricted. Emperors punished dissenters, and open criticism of the government could lead to exile or execution. This pattern showed that while free speech could thrive in democratic settings, it was always at risk when power became too centralized.

The Rise of Modern Rights

The idea of free speech gained momentum during the Enlightenment, a period in the 17th and 18th centuries when thinkers like John Locke, Voltaire, and John Stuart Mill argued that individuals had the right to express their ideas without fear of punishment. These ideas challenged the authority of monarchs and religious institutions, paving the way for democratic revolutions.

Voltaire famously defended free speech with the phrase often attributed to him: "I disapprove of what you say, but I will defend to the death your right to say it." This philosophy laid the foundation for modern democratic societies. Similarly, John Stuart Mill, in his work *On Liberty*, argued that open discourse was essential for progress and that silencing an opinion, even if unpopular, deprived society of the opportunity to seek truth and understanding.

These ideas influenced major political movements, including the American and French Revolutions. In the United States, the First Amendment of the Constitution, ratified in 1791, explicitly protected freedom of speech, ensuring that the government could not silence its citizens. Similarly, the French Declaration of the Rights of Man and of the Citizen in 1789 emphasized the right to free expression. These foundational documents laid the groundwork for modern democratic societies, reinforcing the belief that free speech was essential for progress and justice.

Challenges Through Time

Despite these protections, free speech has faced numerous challenges throughout history. During wartime, governments have often imposed censorship to control public opinion and suppress dissent. For example, during World War I, the U.S. government passed the Espionage Act of 1917, which restricted speech deemed harmful to the war effort. The Sedition Act of 1918 went even further, criminalizing any criticism of the government, military, or war policies. Similar crackdowns occurred in other countries, where critics of war policies were imprisoned or silenced.

During World War II, propaganda was used extensively to shape public perception, and governments censored opposition voices in the name of national security. Even in democratic nations, such as the United Kingdom and the United States, media outlets were restricted in what they could report.

The Cold War era saw another wave of suppression, particularly in the United States during the Red Scare. The McCarthy hearings led to the persecution of individuals accused of communist sympathies, many of whom were blacklisted from their professions without due process. This period demonstrated how fear could be used to justify restrictions on speech, leading to an erosion of civil liberties.

Authoritarian regimes have consistently restricted speech to maintain control. In Nazi Germany, the Soviet Union, and other oppressive states, censorship was used to eliminate opposition and spread propaganda. Books were banned, newspapers were shut down, and dissenters were imprisoned or executed. Even in modern times, countries like China, North Korea, and Russia have implemented strict censorship laws to silence critics and control information.

Lessons from History

History teaches us that free speech must be actively defended. When people accept censorship in the name of security or order, they risk losing their ability to question authority. Many of the rights enjoyed today were won through struggle—by individuals who dared to speak out against injustice, even when it was dangerous to do so. From the abolitionists fighting against slavery to civil rights leaders demanding equality, free speech has been a driving force behind social progress.

The past also shows that no society is immune to the dangers of censorship. Even democracies can slide toward suppression if citizens do not remain vigilant. The rise of political correctness, cancel culture, and corporate control over speech in modern times raises concerns about whether societies are repeating past mistakes. When speech is controlled, whether by the state or powerful private entities, the free exchange of ideas suffers.

By studying history, we can recognize the warning signs and take action to protect free speech before it is too late. Understanding the historical struggles for free speech reminds us of its importance in shaping fair, just, and open societies. The fight for this fundamental right continues, and the lessons of the past can help us preserve it for the future. Free speech is not just a privilege—it is a necessity for democracy and human progress.

CHAPTER 2

Chapter 2: The Rise of Modern Censorship

Censorship by Governments

Governments around the world have long used laws and regulations to control speech, often under the guise of protecting citizens from harm. While some restrictions, such as laws against hate speech or incitement to violence, may be well-intended, many governments use broad and vague language to suppress dissent and silence opposition.

Authoritarian regimes are the most notorious for government-imposed censorship. In countries like China, Russia, and North Korea, strict laws criminalize criticism of the government. The Chinese government, for example, employs the Great Firewall, a massive surveillance and censorship system that blocks access to foreign news, social media, and any content deemed subversive. In Russia, laws against "fake news" have been used to punish journalists and activists who report on government corruption or war efforts.

Even in democratic nations, censorship is on the rise. Laws related to misinformation, extremism, or public safety have been used to justify removing speech deemed controversial. Governments may pressure social media companies to take down content or use emergency powers to limit protests and media coverage. Under the banner of protecting national security, many governments have expanded surveillance programs, monitoring citizens' communications and online activity.

As governments continue to expand their control over digital communication, the line between security and suppression grows thinner. The ability to freely express ideas, challenge policies, and hold leaders accountable is at risk when speech is regulated through vague and politically motivated laws.

Big Tech's Role

In the digital age, social media companies have become the primary gatekeepers of information. Platforms like Facebook, Twitter, and YouTube determine what millions of people see and hear each day. While these companies claim to promote free expression, they also actively moderate content, sometimes in ways that limit free speech.

Social media companies enforce their own policies, banning or restricting content they deem inappropriate. However, these rules are often inconsistently applied, leading to accusations of bias. Certain political views, controversial opinions, or alternative narratives are frequently censored under the pretext of preventing misinformation or hate speech. High-profile cases of deplatforming, where individuals are permanently banned from a platform, demonstrate the immense power these companies wield.

Algorithms further shape what users see, creating echo chambers where individuals are exposed only to content that aligns with their beliefs. This limits open discussion and stifles diverse perspectives, reinforcing ideological divides rather than encouraging meaningful debate. The ability of a handful of companies to decide what information is accessible gives them unprecedented influence over public discourse and political outcomes.

Corporate and Social Pressure

Beyond governments and tech companies, businesses, media outlets, and activist groups play a significant role in enforcing modern censorship. Corporate censorship occurs when companies refuse to associate with individuals or organizations due to their views. Advertisers often pressure media companies and content creators by threatening to pull funding if they publish or broadcast controversial opinions.

The rise of cancel culture has amplified this phenomenon. Public figures, journalists, and ordinary individuals can face severe consequences—including job loss, social ostracization, and threats—simply for expressing unpopular or politically incorrect opinions. Boycotts and online campaigns are frequently used to pressure businesses and platforms into deplatforming individuals or organizations deemed offensive by certain groups.

The media also contributes to censorship by selectively covering or omitting stories that do not align with prevailing narratives. In some cases, biased reporting or fact-checking organizations may discredit or suppress certain perspectives, shaping public perception in a specific direction.

While private companies and social movements have the right to express disapproval, the widespread enforcement of ideological conformity through economic and social pressure creates a chilling effect, discouraging open debate and free thought.

The Hidden Dangers

While some argue that private companies have the right to regulate speech on their platforms, the concentration of power in the hands of a few unelected corporations poses significant risks. When a small number of executives, often with clear political leanings, decide what can and cannot be said, they wield more influence over free speech than many governments.

Censorship often begins with the most extreme voices, but history shows that restrictions inevitably expand to include broader categories of speech. Once mechanisms for silencing dissent are established, they can be used against anyone who challenges prevailing power structures.

Moreover, modern censorship lacks transparency. Many content moderation decisions are made behind closed doors, with little accountability. Users may have their accounts suspended or their content removed without a clear explanation or path for appeal. This lack of due process further erodes trust in digital communication platforms.

The growing partnership between governments, big tech, and media organizations raises additional concerns. When these entities collaborate to suppress speech under the justification of combating misinformation or protecting public safety, it creates an environment where dissent is systematically erased.

To preserve free speech, it is essential to recognize these hidden dangers and advocate for policies that ensure diverse voices can be heard. Transparency in content moderation, decentralization of online platforms, and legal protections for free expression are necessary to prevent the erosion of open discourse and democratic values.

CHAPTER 3

Chapter 3: How Free Speech Protects Democracy

Holding Leaders Accountable

Free speech is one of the most powerful tools for holding leaders accountable. Journalists, activists, and everyday citizens use their voices to expose corruption, challenge injustice, and demand transparency from those in power. Without free speech, governments and institutions can operate without scrutiny, leading to unchecked corruption and abuse of power.

Throughout history, investigative journalism has played a crucial role in uncovering government misconduct. From the Watergate scandal, which led to the resignation of U.S. President Richard Nixon, to reports exposing human rights violations worldwide, courageous journalists have used free speech to bring truth to light. Activists, too, have relied on their right to speak freely to organize protests, advocate for change, and pressure governments to act in the best interest of the people.

When speech is restricted, whistleblowers and truth-tellers face persecution, and citizens are left in the dark about the actions of their leaders. A democracy cannot function if those in power can silence criticism and suppress information that challenges their authority.

Encouraging Open Debate

Democracy thrives on discussion and debate. When people are free to express their opinions, societies benefit from a marketplace of ideas where the best solutions can emerge. Different viewpoints challenge assumptions, force individuals to refine their beliefs, and ultimately lead to better decision-making.

History shows that when speech is stifled, progress slows. Scientific discoveries, social reforms, and political innovations often begin as controversial ideas that face resistance. If Galileo had been permanently silenced for challenging the prevailing views on astronomy, modern science might have been delayed. If civil rights leaders like Martin Luther King Jr. had been prevented from speaking out, the fight for racial equality in America could have taken much longer.

Open debate allows individuals to confront misinformation rather than suppress it. When all perspectives are heard, falsehoods can be exposed and corrected, rather than driven underground where they fester without challenge. In a democracy, free speech ensures that policies and laws reflect the will of an informed public rather than the interests of a select few.

Empowering Individuals

Beyond politics and governance, free speech is essential for personal freedom. The ability to express one's beliefs, ideas, and identity without fear of punishment is a fundamental human right. Free societies allow individuals to speak their minds, practice their faiths, and share their stories without repression.

When speech is controlled, individuals are forced to conform to a single narrative, often dictated by those in power. This suppression stifles creativity, limits innovation, and discourages critical thinking. Artistic expression, literature, and cultural movements all depend on the ability to communicate freely. Throughout history, repressive regimes have sought to silence authors, musicians, and filmmakers whose work challenges the status quo.

Moreover, free speech fosters a sense of agency among citizens. When people feel that their voices matter, they are more likely to engage in civic life, vote in elections, and participate in shaping their communities. A democracy in which citizens are afraid to speak is a democracy in decline.

Preventing Tyranny

One of the clearest lessons from history is that limiting free speech leads to oppression. Authoritarian governments and totalitarian regimes often begin their rise to power by controlling speech, silencing opposition, and manipulating public discourse.

In Nazi Germany, the suppression of dissenting voices allowed the regime to consolidate power and carry out atrocities with little resistance. In the Soviet Union, censorship and propaganda kept citizens in a state of ignorance, preventing them from challenging the government's actions. Modern examples, such as North Korea and China, show how restricting speech allows governments to maintain strict control over their populations.

Democracies are not immune to these dangers. When governments, corporations, or social groups decide what speech is acceptable, they pave the way for authoritarian control. Today, the increasing censorship in the name of safety, misinformation prevention, or political correctness raises concerns about whether democratic nations are moving toward a culture of suppression.

The best way to prevent tyranny is to uphold the principle that all speech, even controversial or unpopular speech, must be protected. The moment a society allows restrictions on speech for the sake of convenience or control, it sets a precedent for further suppression. Free speech is not just an individual right—it is the safeguard that protects democracy itself.

CHAPTER 4

Chapter 4: The Dangers of Political Censorship

Controlling the Narrative

Governments and political groups have long understood the power of controlling information. By shaping the narrative, they can influence public perception, dictate policy discussions, and maintain power. Political censorship is often justified under claims of national security, public order, or the fight against misinformation. However, in many cases, it is simply a means of ensuring that only approved viewpoints reach the public.

State-run media and propaganda machines have historically been used to control narratives. In authoritarian regimes, government-controlled news outlets present a version of reality that aligns with the interests of those in power. Even in democratic societies, selective reporting, editorial bias, and media ownership concentration can create echo chambers that limit the diversity of perspectives available to the public.

Social media platforms have become battlegrounds for narrative control. Algorithms promote certain viewpoints while suppressing others, sometimes without transparency. Governments and political organizations collaborate with tech companies to regulate speech, often labeling dissenting opinions as harmful or misleading. When the flow of information is restricted, citizens are left with a distorted view of reality, unable to make informed decisions about their governance.

Silencing Opponents

One of the most troubling aspects of political censorship is the deliberate suppression of opposition voices. Leaders and ruling parties often use a combination of legal action, media control, and public shaming to stifle dissent.

In many countries, laws against "hate speech" or "fake news" are selectively applied to target political opponents. Journalists, activists, and politicians who challenge the establishment often face harassment, imprisonment, or even violence. In democratic nations, while legal consequences may not be as severe, opposition voices can still be marginalized through biased reporting, deplatforming, and social pressure.

Cancel culture has become a modern tool for silencing those with unpopular opinions. Public figures who express views that go against the dominant political narrative often face professional and personal repercussions. The fear of backlash discourages open debate, creating a climate where only socially acceptable views can be discussed without consequence. When opposition is systematically silenced, the democratic process suffers, as voters are deprived of alternative perspectives.

Manipulating Elections

Free and fair elections are the foundation of democracy, but political censorship undermines the integrity of the electoral process. When information is controlled, voters are unable to make fully informed choices.

Media bias plays a significant role in shaping electoral outcomes. News organizations with political affiliations often give disproportionate coverage to favored candidates while downplaying or negatively framing their opponents. Social media companies, through content moderation and fact-checking policies, can also influence elections by limiting the reach of certain viewpoints.

Censorship of political advertisements, campaign messages, and debates can further manipulate public opinion. If certain candidates or parties are restricted from presenting their platforms, the electorate is left with an incomplete picture of their options. Additionally, political censorship extends to voter suppression efforts, where access to information about voting procedures and candidates is deliberately restricted to benefit specific parties or ideologies.

When political discourse is tightly controlled, elections become less about democratic choice and more about manufactured consent. The ability of a small group of decision-makers to determine what information reaches the public threatens the very essence of free and fair democratic competition.

The Global Threat

Political censorship is not confined to any one country—it is a global phenomenon used by governments and political groups across the world. From authoritarian regimes to democratic societies, controlling speech and information has become a tool for maintaining power and suppressing dissent.

In China, the government's strict censorship policies regulate everything from news to social media conversations, ensuring that only state-approved narratives are allowed. Russia has cracked down on independent journalism, labeling dissenting voices as foreign agents or traitors. In the Middle East, many nations impose strict laws that criminalize political opposition and restrict free expression under the guise of maintaining stability.

Even in democratic nations, increasing collaboration between governments, media outlets, and tech companies has raised concerns about political censorship. Efforts to combat "misinformation" or "extremism" have sometimes led to broad restrictions on legitimate political discourse. As more countries implement policies that restrict speech in the name of social harmony or public safety, the global trend toward political censorship threatens democratic values everywhere.

To protect democracy, it is essential to recognize and resist political censorship in all its forms. Ensuring free speech in politics allows for accountability, informed decision-making, and the preservation of democratic principles. Without it, power becomes concentrated in the hands of those who control information, leaving citizens without the ability to challenge authority or advocate for change.

CHAPTER 5

Chapter 5: The Role of the Media in Censorship

Bias and Agenda-Setting

Major news outlets play a crucial role in shaping public opinion, but many do so by pushing specific narratives while suppressing opposing viewpoints. Instead of presenting balanced coverage, media organizations often promote stories that align with their ideological or financial interests, leaving out critical perspectives that challenge the prevailing discourse.

Agenda-setting theory suggests that the media doesn't tell people what to think but rather what to think about. By selectively covering certain topics and ignoring others, news organizations can influence public perception and priorities. For example, some issues may receive extensive coverage while others are downplayed or ignored entirely, creating a distorted view of reality.

News bias is further reinforced by editorial decisions, the choice of sources, and the framing of stories. Loaded language, emotional appeals, and selective reporting can manipulate how audiences interpret events. When media outlets act as gatekeepers of information, the public is left with an incomplete understanding of critical issues, which can influence elections, policy decisions, and social attitudes.

The Rise of Fact-Checking

In recent years, the rise of fact-checking organizations has added a new layer to media censorship. While fact-checking was originally intended to promote truth and accuracy, it has increasingly been used as a tool to control narratives and discredit certain viewpoints.

Many fact-checking organizations are funded by large corporations, political groups, or governments, raising concerns about bias. When fact-checkers selectively label information as "misleading" or "false," they often do so based on subjective interpretations rather than indisputable facts. This allows them to silence dissenting voices under the guise of combating misinformation.

Furthermore, fact-checking can be weaponized to limit public debate. By labeling certain discussions as "harmful" or "dangerous," platforms and media outlets justify the removal of content, deplatforming individuals, or demonetizing independent voices. In some cases, legitimate discussions on controversial topics have been censored simply because they challenge mainstream narratives. Instead of fostering open discourse, fact-checking has increasingly become a mechanism for information control.

Censorship of Independent Journalism

Independent journalists and whistleblowers play a crucial role in uncovering corruption, exposing misconduct, and providing alternative perspectives. However, these voices are often targeted for revealing inconvenient truths that powerful entities would rather keep hidden.

Traditional media organizations, which once prided themselves on investigative journalism, now often dismiss or attack independent reporters. When mainstream media outlets serve corporate or political interests, they have little incentive to promote stories that challenge their benefactors. As a result, independent journalists are frequently labeled as "conspiracy theorists," "extremists," or "misinformation spreaders" to undermine their credibility.

Whistleblowers who expose government or corporate wrongdoing also face significant risks. Figures like Edward Snowden, Julian Assange, and others have been persecuted for revealing classified information that exposed unethical practices. Instead of being celebrated for holding power to account, these individuals are often vilified, prosecuted, or forced into exile. The suppression of independent journalism creates an environment where only sanctioned narratives are allowed, making it harder for the public to access diverse and truthful information.

The Death of Objective News

As media censorship intensifies, the concept of objective news is rapidly fading. Journalism, once valued for its commitment to impartiality and factual reporting, has increasingly shifted toward advocacy and propaganda. When media outlets function as extensions of political or corporate interests, the public is deprived of fair and accurate reporting.

The blurring of news and opinion has become a significant problem. Many media organizations present opinion-based analysis as objective reporting, leading audiences to mistake biased perspectives for facts. This shift has created a deeply polarized media landscape where people consume news not to be informed, but to reinforce their existing beliefs.

Additionally, censorship and media bias contribute to growing distrust in journalism. When people perceive that the news is being manipulated or filtered, they turn to alternative sources, some of which may indeed spread misinformation. This cycle erodes public trust in traditional media and fuels greater division.

For a democracy to function properly, citizens need access to reliable and unbiased information. The more media censorship grows, the closer society moves toward a controlled and manipulated flow of information, where truth becomes secondary to political and financial interests. Reclaiming objective journalism is essential to ensuring that free speech and democratic values remain intact.

CHAPTER 6

Chapter 6: Social Media and the Digital Battle for

The Power of Big Tech

Social media platforms like Facebook, Twitter, and YouTube have become the primary spaces for public discussion, making them incredibly influential in shaping opinions and controlling the flow of information. Unlike traditional news outlets, which are subject to journalistic standards and public scrutiny, these tech giants operate with minimal oversight, allowing them to decide what content is permitted and what is banned.

Big Tech companies often justify their censorship by citing community guidelines, terms of service, or the need to prevent misinformation and hate speech. However, these policies are often applied inconsistently, with some viewpoints being aggressively suppressed while others are given free rein. This power to moderate content gives these corporations unprecedented control over political discourse, social movements, and even election outcomes.

When platforms remove content or ban users, it doesn't just affect those individuals—it shapes the entire public conversation. By limiting access to certain viewpoints, Big Tech effectively determines what narratives dominate online spaces, influencing what people believe and how they engage with critical issues.

The Algorithms of Control

Beyond direct censorship, social media platforms use hidden algorithms to control what users see. These algorithms determine which posts appear on news feeds, which videos are recommended, and which voices get amplified or suppressed.

Algorithmic bias can be a powerful form of censorship because it operates invisibly. Users may not realize that certain perspectives are being suppressed because they simply never see them. For example, a platform's algorithm may promote content that aligns with mainstream narratives while burying or limiting the reach of dissenting views. This creates digital echo chambers, where users are repeatedly exposed to the same ideas while alternative perspectives remain hidden.

Additionally, tech companies frequently tweak these algorithms to favor corporate partners, advertisers, or political interests. The result is a curated digital environment where what people perceive as organic discourse is, in fact, carefully engineered to serve specific agendas.

Deplatforming and Shadow Banning

One of the most insidious forms of online censorship is deplatforming, where individuals or organizations are completely removed from social media platforms, often without clear justification. High-profile figures, journalists, and even ordinary users have found themselves banned for expressing controversial opinions, even when their content does not violate explicit platform rules.

Even more subtle is shadow banning—a practice where a user's content remains visible to them but is deliberately restricted from reaching a wider audience. Unlike outright bans, shadow banning allows platforms to silence individuals without making it obvious, preventing backlash while still controlling the conversation.

These tactics disproportionately affect those with dissenting views, particularly on politically sensitive topics. Many users only realize they've been shadow banned when they notice a sudden drop in engagement, a lack of visibility on search results, or an inability to interact with their followers effectively. By using these silent methods, Big Tech can suppress speech while avoiding accusations of outright censorship.

Can Tech Be Fixed?

With social media playing such a central role in modern communication, the question remains: can the digital battle for free speech be won? While tech giants continue to consolidate power, alternative platforms and legal solutions are emerging to challenge their dominance.

Some platforms, such as Rumble, Gab, and Truth Social, have positioned themselves as free speech-friendly alternatives to mainstream social media. While these sites offer refuge for censored voices, they often struggle with scalability, monetization, and mainstream adoption.

Legal battles over online censorship are also gaining traction, with governments and advocacy groups pushing for stronger free speech protections in digital spaces. Some argue that social media platforms should be treated as public utilities, subject to regulations that prevent viewpoint discrimination. Others advocate for clearer content moderation policies that ensure fairness and transparency.

Ultimately, the fight for free speech in the digital age is far from over. As technology continues to evolve, so must the efforts to protect open dialogue and prevent centralized control over public discourse. The choices made today will determine whether the internet remains a space for free expression or becomes an increasingly controlled and censored landscape.

CHAPTER 7

Chapter 7: Hate Speech vs. Free Speech

Defining Hate Speech

Hate speech is often broadly defined as speech that expresses hatred, discrimination, or incites violence against a particular group based on race, religion, gender, or other characteristics. While this definition may seem straightforward, the problem arises in determining who decides what qualifies as hate speech.

Different countries, institutions, and social groups have varying definitions, making the concept highly subjective. What one person sees as a valid critique, another may perceive as offensive or hateful. This subjectivity makes it difficult to enforce hate speech regulations fairly and consistently.

Furthermore, cultural and political differences influence how hate speech is interpreted. In some countries, political dissent is labeled as hate speech to suppress opposition, while in others, strong religious or ideological beliefs are categorized as hateful simply for challenging mainstream views. Without a clear and universal standard, hate speech laws risk being used as tools for ideological control rather than for the protection of marginalized groups.

The Problem with Banning Speech

While the idea of banning hate speech may seem like a step toward a more inclusive society, history has shown that speech restrictions often lead to unintended consequences. One major problem is that such restrictions can quickly evolve into political and ideological censorship.

Governments and powerful institutions have used hate speech laws to silence dissenting voices, censor controversial opinions, and punish those who challenge authority. When speech restrictions become overly broad, they no longer protect people from harm but instead serve as a weapon against free expression.

For instance, laws originally designed to prevent racial or religious discrimination have, in some cases, been used to criminalize political speech or silence discussions on sensitive topics. Instead of fostering open dialogue, banning speech creates fear, self-censorship, and a society where individuals hesitate to express their views.

Slippery Slope to Tyranny

History has repeatedly demonstrated that restricting speech in the name of combating hate can lead to authoritarian control. Once the power to define and regulate speech is placed in the hands of governments, corporations, or activist groups, it is only a matter of time before those regulations are used to suppress opposition.

Totalitarian regimes throughout history have justified censorship by claiming they were protecting society from dangerous ideas. The Soviet Union, Nazi Germany, and other oppressive governments controlled speech under the pretext of maintaining order and unity. What began as restrictions on harmful speech quickly escalated into widespread censorship, persecution, and loss of individual freedoms.

Even in modern democratic societies, the gradual expansion of hate speech laws has led to increased limitations on public discourse. When free speech is restricted to avoid offending others, society loses its ability to engage in honest and necessary discussions. The more power authorities have to regulate speech, the greater the risk of tyranny creeping in under the guise of social protection.

Alternative Solutions

Rather than banning speech, society should focus on alternative ways to combat hate while preserving free expression. Education, open debate, and social accountability are far more effective in addressing hateful ideas than outright censorship.

Promoting media literacy and critical thinking skills allows people to challenge harmful ideas rather than suppress them. Encouraging open conversations enables individuals to engage with opposing viewpoints and counter hate with reason and evidence. When speech is openly debated, destructive ideologies can be exposed and dismantled rather than hidden in the shadows where they may fester unchecked.

Additionally, social pressure and voluntary action can serve as effective tools against hate. Communities, businesses, and organizations can choose to disassociate from harmful rhetoric without relying on government-mandated restrictions. Rather than empowering authorities to decide what speech is acceptable, individuals and private institutions can take responsibility for promoting respectful dialogue and rejecting discrimination without infringing on fundamental freedoms.

In the end, the best way to combat hate is not through censorship but through an open, informed, and engaged society that values free speech as a fundamental pillar of democracy.

CHAPTER 8

Chapter 8: The Global War on Free Speech

Authoritarian Censorship

Throughout history, authoritarian regimes have relied on strict censorship to maintain control over their populations. In countries like China, Russia, and Iran, free speech is heavily restricted to suppress dissent and ensure government authority remains unchallenged.

China's Great Firewall is one of the most sophisticated censorship systems in the world, blocking access to foreign news, social media platforms, and any content critical of the Communist Party. Journalists, activists, and even ordinary citizens face imprisonment for expressing views that go against state-approved narratives. The Chinese government employs mass surveillance, artificial intelligence, and harsh punishments to ensure compliance, making free expression nearly impossible.

Russia has also tightened its grip on free speech, particularly under Vladimir Putin's leadership. Independent media outlets have been shut down, journalists critical of the government have been imprisoned or assassinated, and new laws criminalize "fake news"—a term often used to silence opposition. Social media platforms are closely monitored, and those who spread anti-government messages risk severe consequences.

In Iran, the government enforces strict speech laws based on religious and political ideology. Protests are violently suppressed, online platforms are censored, and critics of the regime are frequently arrested or executed. The government uses morality laws to justify speech restrictions, making it dangerous for citizens to express opinions that challenge Islamic rule.

These examples highlight how authoritarian governments weaponize censorship to maintain their grip on power, suppress opposition, and control the flow of information.

Western Censorship Trends

While democratic nations have long championed free speech, recent trends show a growing tendency toward censorship in the name of safety, inclusivity, and misinformation prevention. Governments and private organizations in the West are increasingly using laws and policies to regulate speech, often under the guise of protecting the public.

In Europe, hate speech laws have expanded significantly, with countries like Germany, France, and the UK penalizing individuals for offensive or politically incorrect speech. Social media companies are required to remove "illegal" content quickly, but these vague laws often result in the suppression of legitimate political debate and controversial opinions.

In the United States, free speech is protected under the First Amendment, but social pressure, corporate censorship, and political influence have created an environment where certain viewpoints are silenced. Tech companies, universities, and media outlets frequently ban or deplatform individuals who express unpopular opinions, creating an unofficial but powerful form of censorship.

Australia and Canada have also introduced policies aimed at combating “harmful” speech, including online regulation bills that give the government broad power to remove content deemed offensive or misleading. While these measures are often justified as necessary to prevent harm, they raise concerns about overreach and the erosion of free expression.

The Rise of Speech Laws

New speech laws are emerging around the world, limiting public discussion on controversial topics such as politics, gender identity, religion, and history. These laws, often framed as protections against misinformation, extremism, or hate speech, can have far-reaching consequences for free expression.

For example, laws targeting "misinformation" on COVID-19 led to widespread removal of content questioning government policies, even when those questions were later proven valid. Similarly, laws restricting speech on gender and identity issues have resulted in fines and legal action against individuals who express traditional or religious views.

Blasphemy laws remain in effect in several countries, criminalizing criticism of religious figures or institutions. In some places, speaking against religious doctrine can lead to imprisonment or even death, showing how speech laws are often used to uphold ideological control rather than protect individuals.

With the rise of artificial intelligence and automated moderation, governments and corporations now have more tools than ever to monitor, filter, and suppress speech on a massive scale. The combination of legal restrictions, technological advancements, and social pressure makes it increasingly difficult for individuals to speak freely without fear of retribution.

Fighting Back Globally

Despite the increasing restrictions on free speech, individuals and organizations around the world are fighting back to preserve open dialogue and resist censorship.

Organizations like the Electronic Frontier Foundation (EFF) and Reporters Without Borders work tirelessly to defend digital rights, protect journalists, and challenge government censorship. Free speech activists and independent media outlets continue to push back against restrictive laws, often at great personal risk.

In some countries, underground networks and encrypted communication platforms allow people to bypass censorship and share information freely. Tools like VPNs and decentralized social media platforms have become essential for those seeking to evade government surveillance and control.

Legal challenges to speech restrictions are also gaining momentum. In the United States, lawsuits against tech companies and government agencies aim to hold them accountable for suppressing speech. International human rights groups continue to advocate for stronger protections against censorship in both authoritarian and democratic countries.

While the battle for free speech is far from over, the global resistance against censorship proves that people around the world value their right to express themselves. By staying informed, supporting free speech organizations, and pushing back against restrictive policies, individuals can help ensure that the fundamental right to free expression is preserved for future generations.

CHAPTER 9

Chapter 9: Free Speech and the Culture Wars

Cancel Culture and Public Shaming

Cancel culture has emerged as a powerful force in modern society, where individuals face severe consequences for expressing controversial or unpopular opinions. Social media platforms amplify public outrage, turning minor missteps or differing viewpoints into grounds for professional and social punishment.

High-profile cases have shown how individuals—whether celebrities, academics, or everyday people—can be "canceled" for past statements, jokes, or even private conversations. Employers often bow to social pressure, firing employees over perceived offenses, while publishers, streaming platforms, and universities sever ties with those deemed problematic.

While some argue that cancel culture is a form of accountability, others warn that it fosters fear and suppresses open discussion. Instead of engaging in debate, people self-censor to avoid backlash, leading to a chilling effect on free expression. The danger of cancel culture is not just in punishing those with extreme views but in making even reasonable discourse risky.

The Battle on College Campuses

Universities have long been considered havens for intellectual exploration and free debate. However, in recent years, many institutions have shifted towards restricting speech in the name of inclusivity and emotional safety.

Speakers invited to discuss controversial topics often face protests, disruptions, or outright bans. Student groups pressure administrations to deplatform individuals whose views they oppose, claiming that certain ideas create an unsafe learning environment. Even professors have been disciplined or dismissed for challenging prevailing campus ideologies.

Speech codes and bias response teams have further contributed to an environment where students and faculty are hesitant to express dissenting opinions. Some universities have implemented "safe spaces" and trigger warnings, reinforcing the idea that difficult conversations should be avoided rather than confronted.

This trend raises concerns about the future of academic freedom. If universities suppress debate rather than encourage it, students graduate without the ability to engage critically with opposing ideas—an essential skill for a functioning democracy.

Speech vs. Feelings

A key debate in modern culture is whether offensive or harmful speech should be restricted to protect individuals' emotional well-being. Some argue that certain types of speech, particularly those perceived as hateful or discriminatory, should be curtailed to prevent psychological harm. Others believe that the very essence of free speech is the ability to express ideas, even if they offend.

The concept of "microaggressions"—small, often unintended comments that may be perceived as offensive—has fueled policies aimed at policing speech. Workplace diversity programs, social media guidelines, and campus speech codes increasingly emphasize emotional impact over intent.

However, placing subjective feelings at the center of speech regulations presents serious challenges. What one person finds offensive, another may see as honest discourse. Once speech is restricted based on hurt feelings, the line between acceptable and unacceptable speech becomes arbitrary and ever-changing.

The Need for Tough Conversations

A free society requires the ability to discuss difficult and even uncomfortable topics. While it is natural to want to avoid offense, shielding people from controversial ideas does more harm than good. Progress in civil rights, science, and politics has always come from challenging prevailing norms, which is only possible when people are allowed to speak freely.

Difficult conversations about race, gender, religion, and politics are necessary for understanding and growth. If certain perspectives are deemed too controversial to discuss, societies risk stagnation, division, and resentment. Free speech fosters resilience, encouraging individuals to engage with challenging ideas rather than retreat from them.

Instead of silencing voices, society should focus on promoting open dialogue, critical thinking, and respectful debate. The solution to offensive speech is more speech—not censorship. By defending free expression, we ensure that all ideas, including those that challenge our own, have a place in public discourse.

CHAPTER 10

Chapter 10: How to Defend Free Speech

Know Your Rights

Understanding free speech protections is the first step in defending them. In many democratic nations, free speech is protected by law—such as the First Amendment in the United States—ensuring that individuals can express their opinions without government interference. However, these protections have limits, such as speech that incites violence or defamation.

It is crucial for individuals to educate themselves about what is and isn't legally protected speech. Misconceptions about free speech often lead to confusion, with people believing they have a right to be heard on private platforms or that criticism equals censorship. Knowing the legal framework helps individuals advocate effectively and recognize true violations of free speech.

Additionally, organizations like the ACLU, FIRE, and other legal groups offer resources and support for those whose speech rights are under threat. Being informed empowers people to defend their own rights and assist others facing suppression.

Supporting Open Platforms

With Big Tech controlling much of today's communication, it is essential to support platforms that value free expression. Many mainstream social media companies enforce restrictive content policies, silencing voices based on subjective guidelines.

Alternatives such as decentralized platforms, blockchain-based networks, and independent media outlets provide spaces for unrestricted dialogue. Users can promote free speech by choosing services that prioritize open discourse and transparency.

Additionally, advocating for platform neutrality—where digital services remain open to all perspectives without political or ideological bias—can help shift the online landscape. Supporting businesses and organizations that resist censorship helps create a competitive marketplace for ideas.

Challenging Censorship

Individuals can take action against censorship in government, media, and business through several means. First, calling out censorship when it occurs—whether through social media, petitions, or direct advocacy—raises awareness and puts pressure on decision-makers.

Legal challenges have also played a significant role in rolling back restrictions on speech. By supporting lawsuits that challenge unconstitutional censorship, individuals can help establish important legal precedents.

Boycotting companies that engage in censorship and supporting those that uphold free speech values is another powerful tool. Consumers influence corporate policies through their choices, and businesses respond to market demands.

Lastly, engaging with elected officials and advocating for stronger free speech protections can lead to policy changes. Laws that prevent government overreach in regulating speech, as well as measures that ensure transparency in online content moderation, are critical for maintaining open discourse.

Building a Free Speech Culture

Defending free speech is not just about laws and policies—it's about fostering a culture where diverse opinions are respected. Encouraging open dialogue in schools, workplaces, and public forums ensures that society remains receptive to different viewpoints.

Teaching young people the importance of free expression, critical thinking, and debate prepares future generations to uphold these values. Schools and universities should be places of discussion, not censorship, and parents should encourage children to engage with differing opinions rather than avoid them.

Respectful discourse should be promoted, even when opinions clash. Civility does not require agreement, but it does require a willingness to listen and engage. By defending the right of all people to speak freely, we safeguard democracy and ensure that the marketplace of ideas remains vibrant and diverse.

Conclusion: The Fight for the Future

The Cost of Silence

When free speech is restricted, the consequences ripple throughout society. Suppression of ideas leads to a lack of innovation, silences dissent, and gives unchecked power to those in control. History has shown that societies that restrict speech often descend into authoritarianism, where truth is dictated rather than discovered.

Censorship stifles debate, preventing people from discussing and resolving critical issues. Without open discourse, misinformation flourishes, and people grow distrustful of institutions that claim to protect them. Furthermore, when individuals fear speaking out, they self-censor, allowing dangerous ideas to go unchallenged. The cost of silence is high, leading to a world where only approved narratives can exist.

Why Every Voice Matters

Throughout history, ordinary people have played a vital role in defending free speech. From whistleblowers exposing corruption to activists fighting oppressive laws, change has always started with individuals who refuse to be silenced. Figures like Martin Luther King Jr., Václav Havel, and many others have demonstrated the power of speech in shaping societies.

Even today, people who speak out against censorship—whether through protests, journalism, or social media—contribute to the preservation of free discourse. Every person has a voice, and using it to challenge injustice, spread awareness, and advocate for open dialogue strengthens democracy. The fight for free speech isn't just for lawmakers or journalists; it belongs to everyone.

A Call to Action

Protecting free speech requires active participation. Readers can take several steps to defend this fundamental right:

- **Stay informed** – Understanding how censorship operates allows individuals to recognize and resist it.
- **Support free speech organizations** – Groups that fight for speech rights rely on public backing to challenge unjust restrictions.
- **Engage in open discourse** – Encouraging respectful debates and refusing to participate in cancel culture helps create a free speech-friendly environment.
- **Hold leaders accountable** – Politicians and corporate leaders must hear from citizens who demand free expression.
- **Use alternative platforms** – Supporting free speech-friendly media and technology helps counterbalance restrictive spaces.

Taking even small steps makes a difference. A culture that values free speech is built through the everyday actions of individuals willing to stand up for their right—and the right of others—to speak freely.

A Hopeful Future

Despite the challenges, the battle for free speech is not lost. Awareness is growing, and more people are recognizing the dangers of unchecked censorship. Efforts to create alternative platforms, push for fairer policies, and challenge speech restrictions in court are gaining momentum.

With persistence, open dialogue, and collective action, free speech can be protected and even strengthened. History has shown that freedom, once threatened, can be reclaimed when people rise to defend it. The future of free speech depends on those willing to fight for it, ensuring that generations to come will inherit a world where ideas can be freely expressed, challenged, and refined.

The fight for free speech is the fight for democracy itself. And it's a fight worth winning.

Enjoyed This Book? Let Others Know!

If this book has blessed, encouraged, or challenged you in any way, I'd love to hear about it! Your review not only helps others discover this message but also encourages me to keep writing.

Would you take a moment to share your thoughts? A few sentences on what stood out to you can make a big difference.

You can leave a review on Amazon, Goodreads, or wherever you purchased this book. Thank you for being part of this journey!

www.ingramcontent.com/pod-product-compliance
Lightning Source LLC
LaVergne TN
LVHW090336210926
848480LV00004B/1428
* 9 7 9 8 3 4 9 2 3 5 4 1 2 *